THE FABER MUSIC THEATRE SONGBOOK

18 classic show songs for voice and piano with guitar chords

Compiled by Lin Marsh

FABER ff MUSIC

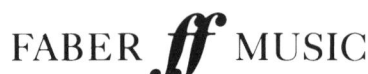

Foreword

The musical is one of the most enjoyable and accessible of theatrical experiences, for performers and audience alike. Every school puts on a show, every town has an amateur operatic or musical society, and taking part in such performances often remains a highlight in the memory. But the specially chosen songs in this collection work well in their own right too, whether for auditions, karaoke, or to share with friends.

Featuring such all-time classic shows as *Cabaret*, *42nd Street* and *Singin' in the Rain*, to more modern hits such as *The Lion King*, *Beauty and the Beast* and *Rent* – these songs are suitable for all ages. Before learning any of the songs, try to understand the musical style of the show. Where and when is it set? Is it classical, mainstream, jazz, cabaret, or rock/pop in style? Does the singing require an accent/dialect of any sort? The synopses provided at the back of the book will help put the songs in context, and the fun backing tracks will be useful for rehearsing, performing, or simply to sing along with wherever you are!

Lin Marsh

© 2008 by Faber Music Ltd
First published in 2008 by Faber Music Ltd
Bloomsbury House
74–77 Great Russell Street
London WC1B 3DA
Cover design by Lydia Merrills-Ashcroft
Printed in England by Caligraving Ltd
All rights reserved

ISBN: 0-571-52610-1
EAN: 978-0-571-52610-9

Backing tracks created and engineered by Olly Wedgwood
Produced by Leigh Rumsey
℗ 2008 Faber Music Ltd © 2008 Faber Music Ltd

To buy Faber Music publications or to find out about the full range of titles available
please contact your local retailer or Faber Music sales enquiries:

Faber Music Limited, Burnt Mill, Elizabeth Way, Harlow CM20 2HX England
Tel: +44 (0) 1279 82 89 82
fabermusic.com

Contents

Title	Backing track	Page
Forty-Second Street from *42nd Street* — Harry Warren and Al Dubin	1	4
Circle of Life from *The Lion King* — Elton John and Tim Rice	2	8
Chim Chim Cher-ee from *Mary Poppins* — Richard Sherman and Robert Sherman	3	12
Sunrise, Sunset from *Fiddler on the Roof* — Sheldon Harnick and Jerry Bock	4	16
Skimbleshanks: the Railway Cat from *Cats* — Thomas Eliot and Andrew Lloyd Webber	5	20
Cabaret from *Cabaret* — John Kander and Fred Ebb	6	29
Hernando's Hideaway from *The Pajama Game* — Richard Adler	7	32
Summer Nights from *Grease* — Jim Jacobs and Warren Casey	8	35
Singin' in the Rain from *Singin' in the Rain* — Arthur Freed and Nacio Brown	9	40
You're Never Fully Dressed Without a Smile from *Annie* — Martin Charnin and Charles Strouse	10	42
Comedy Tonight from *A Funny Thing Happened on the Way to the Forum* — Stephen Sondheim	11	45
Come Follow the Band from *Barnum* — Cy Coleman and Michael Stewart	12	48
Corner of the Sky from *Pippin* — Stephen Schwartz	13	55
Beauty and the Beast from *Beauty and the Beast* — Howard Ashman and Alan Menken	14	60
Seasons of Love from *Rent* — Jonathan Larson	15	64
And All That Jazz from *Chicago* — John Kander and Fred Ebb	16	70
We Go Together from *Grease* — Warren Casey and Jim Jacobs	17	78
Flash, Bang, Wallop! from *Half a Sixpence* — David Heneker	18	83
Synopses of the shows		86

To download the audio tracks scan the QR code or go to fabermusic.com/audio.

Forty-Second Street

from *42nd Street*

Words by Al Dubin
Music by Harry Warren
arr. Lin Marsh

© 1932 M Witmark & Sons
B Feldman & Co Ltd

8

Circle of Life
from *The Lion King*

vocal range

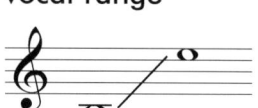

Words by Tim Rice
Music by Elton John
arr. Lin Marsh

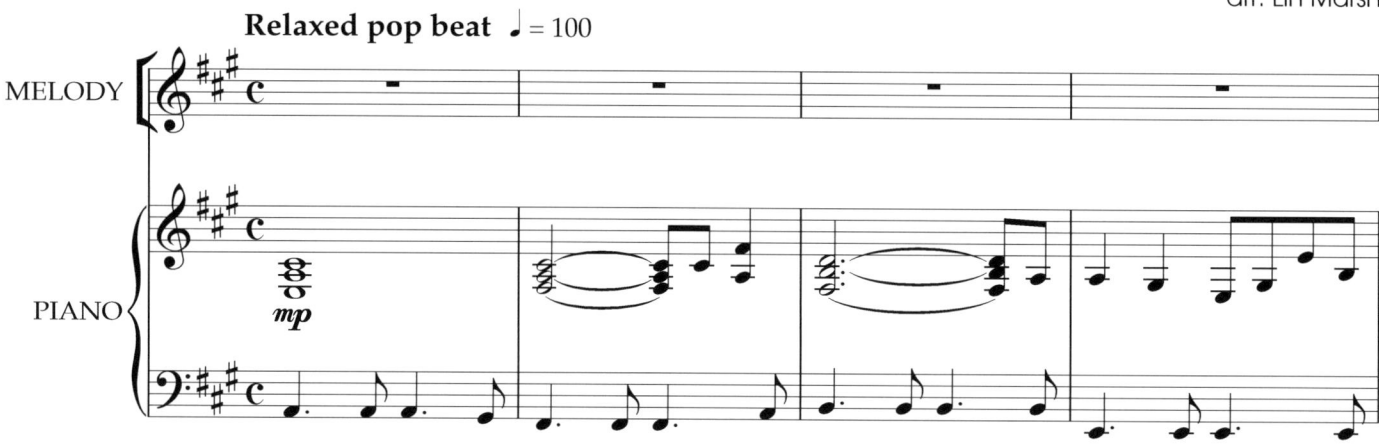

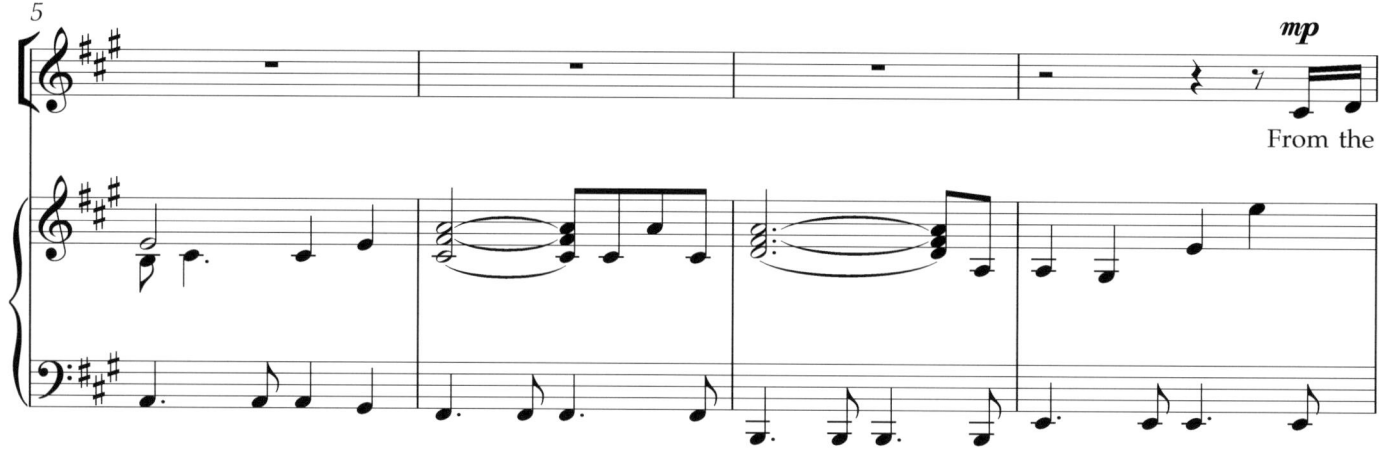

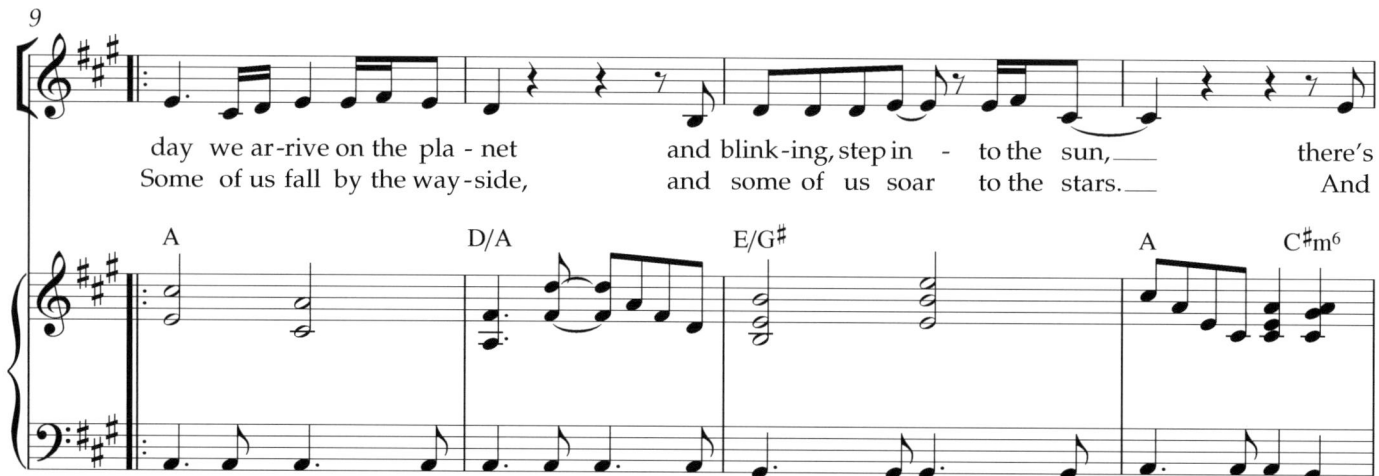

© 1994 WonderLand Music Company Inc
Warner/Chappell Artemis Ltd

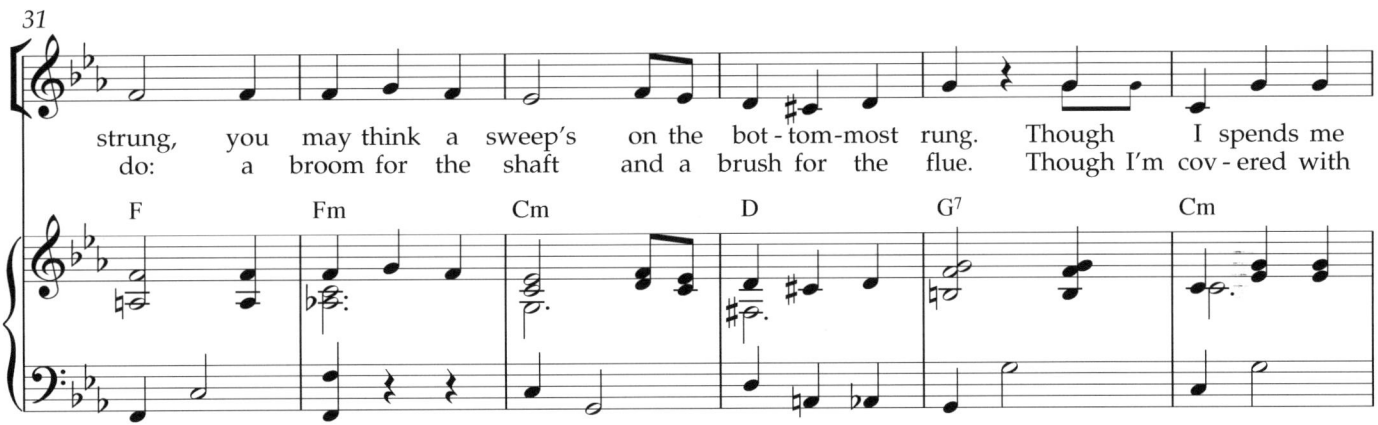
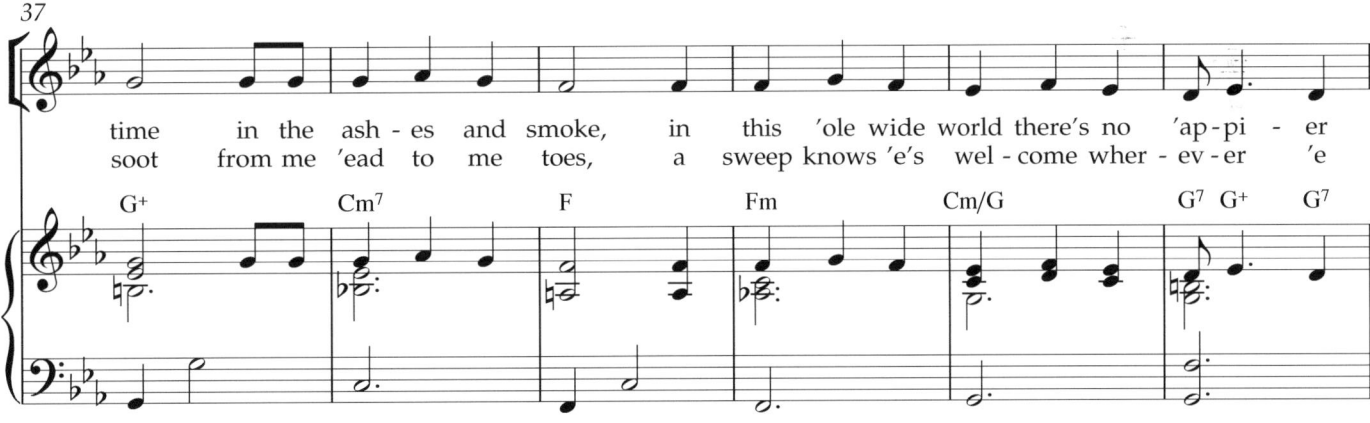

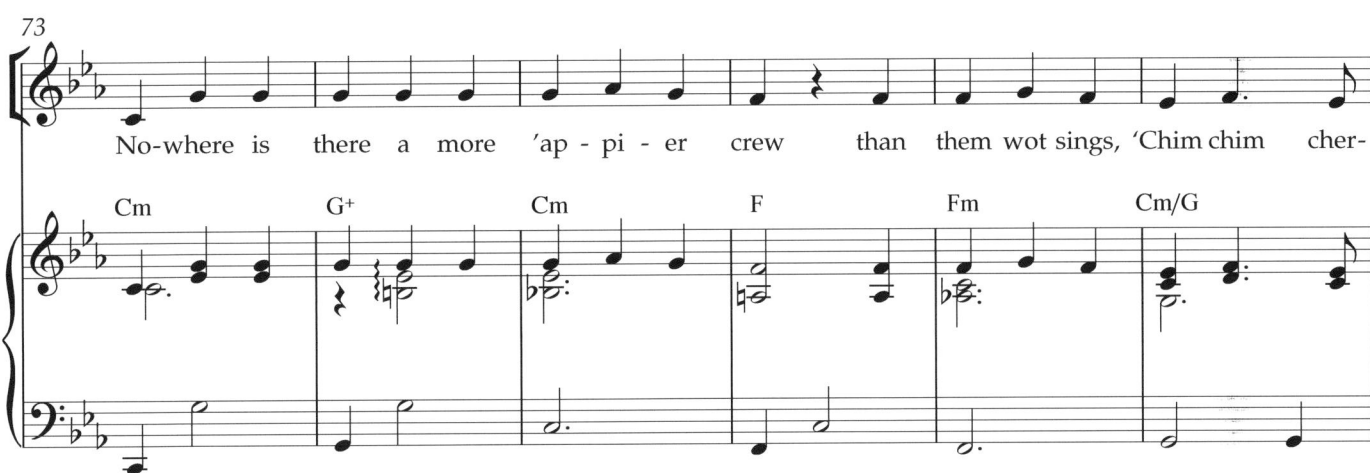

Sunrise, Sunset

from *Fiddler on the Roof*

Words by Sheldon Harnick
Music by Jerry Bock
arr. Lin Marsh

vocal range

Moderately slow waltz tempo ♩ = 116

1. Is this the lit-tle girl I car - - ried?
2. Now is the lit-tle boy a bride - - groom,

Gm   D⁷   Gm

Is this the lit-tle boy at play?   I don't re-
Now is the lit-tle girl a bride.   Un-der the
D⁷   Gm   G⁷   Cm

-mem-ber grow-ing old - - er,   When did
can-o-py I see   them,   Side by
G⁷   Cm   A   A⁷

© 1964 Alley Music Corp, Trio Music Co Inc and Jerry Bock Enterprises Ltd
Carlin Music Corp

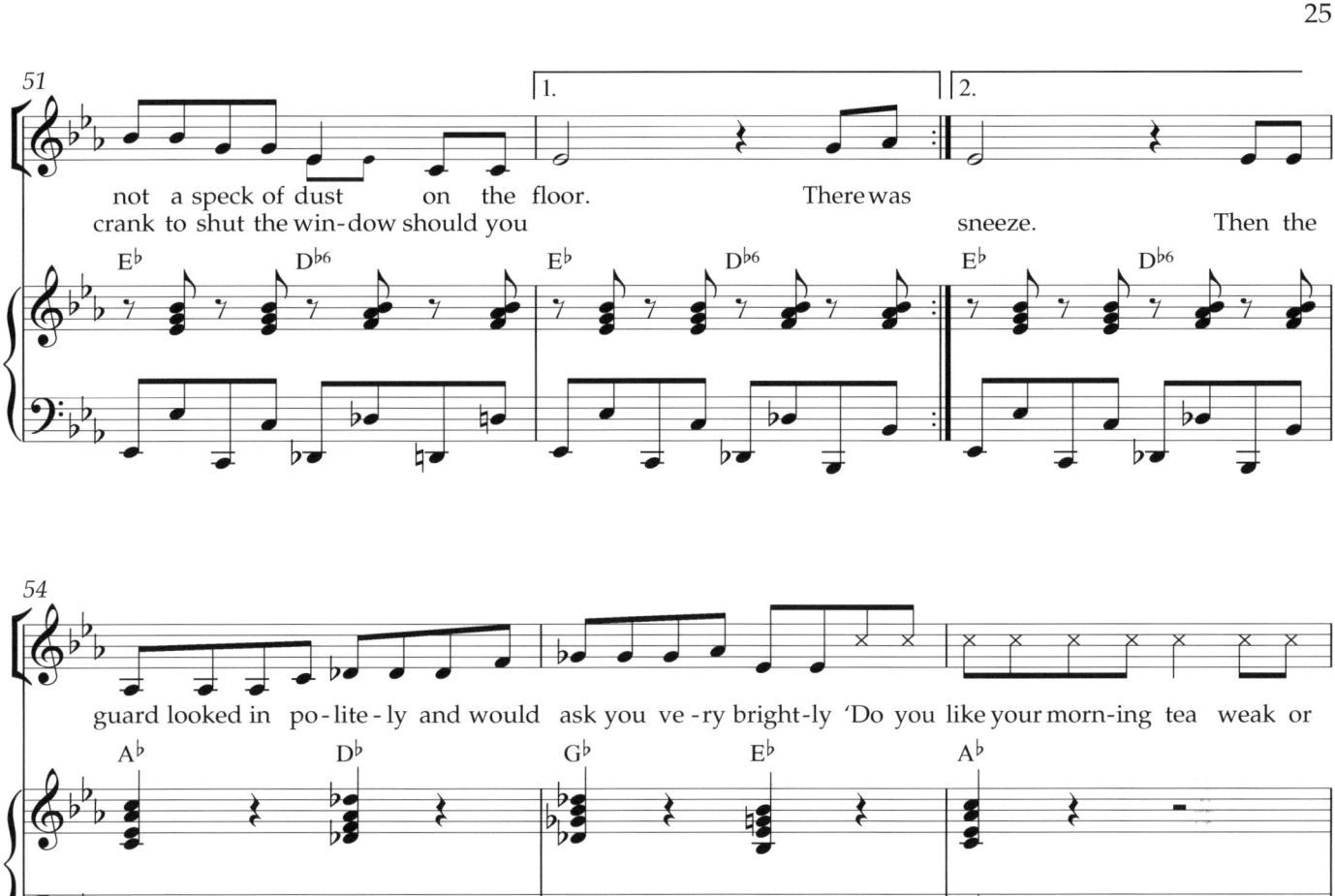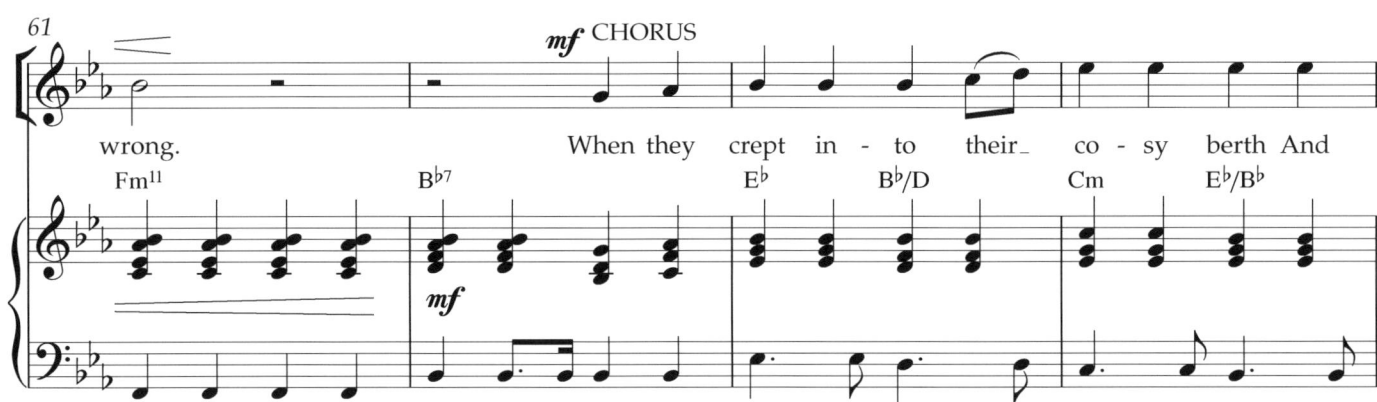

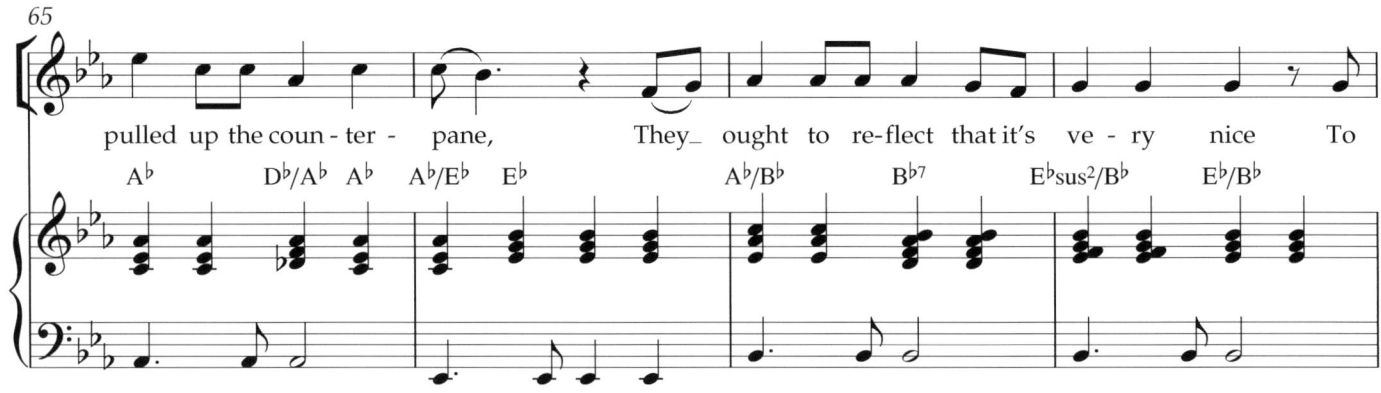
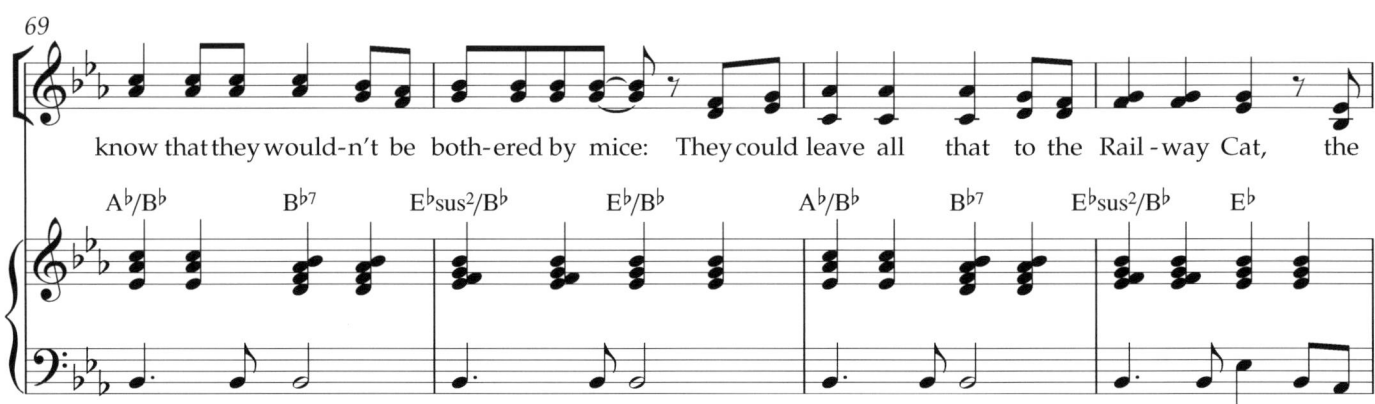

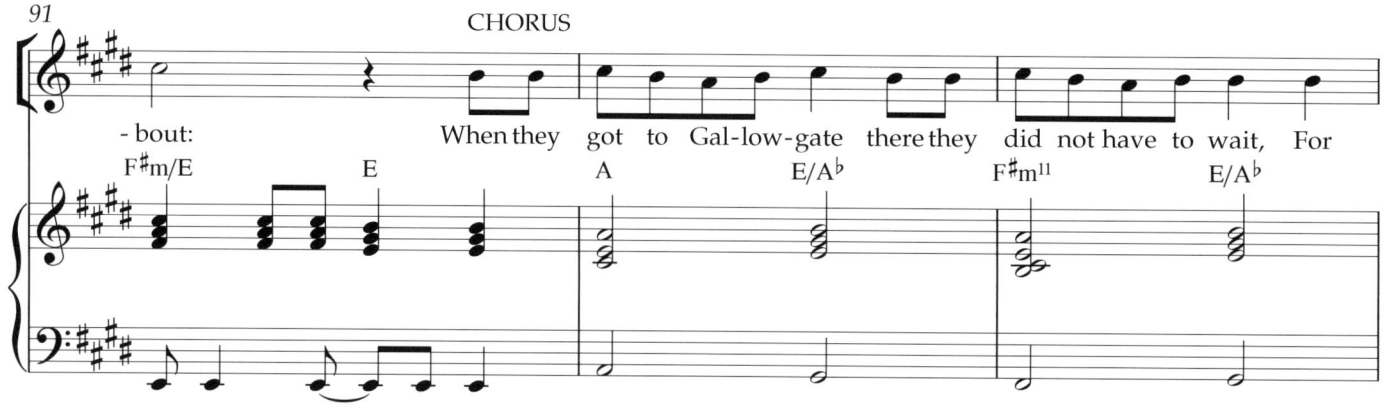

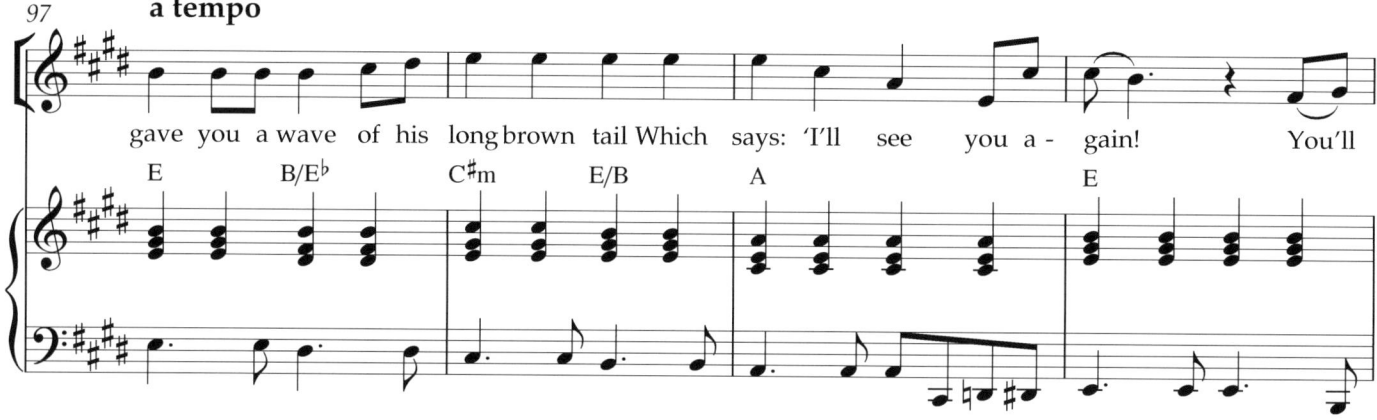
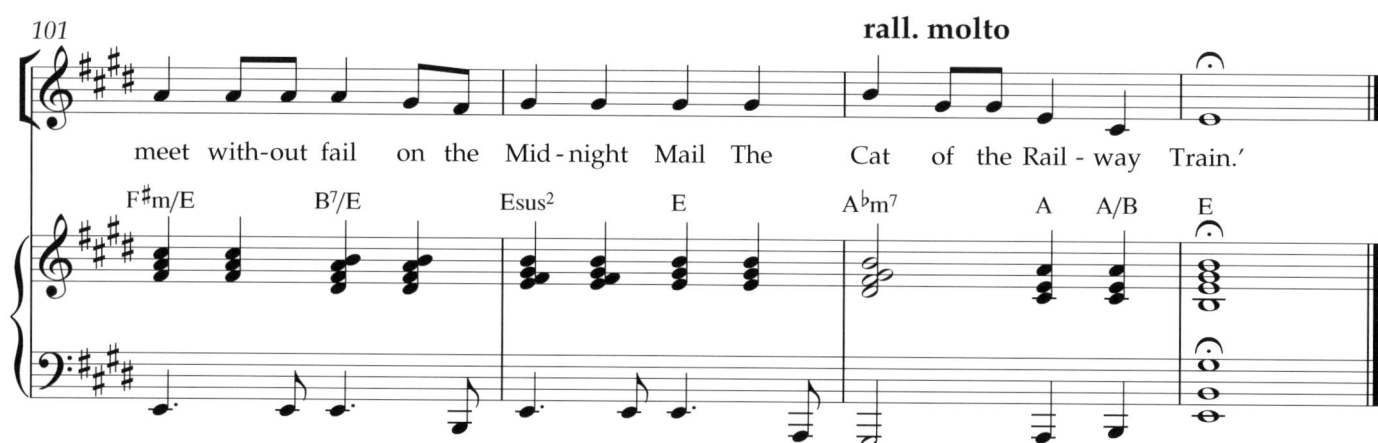

Hernando's Hideaway

from *The Pajama Game*

vocal range

Words and Music by
Richard Adler and Jerry Ross
arr. Lin Marsh

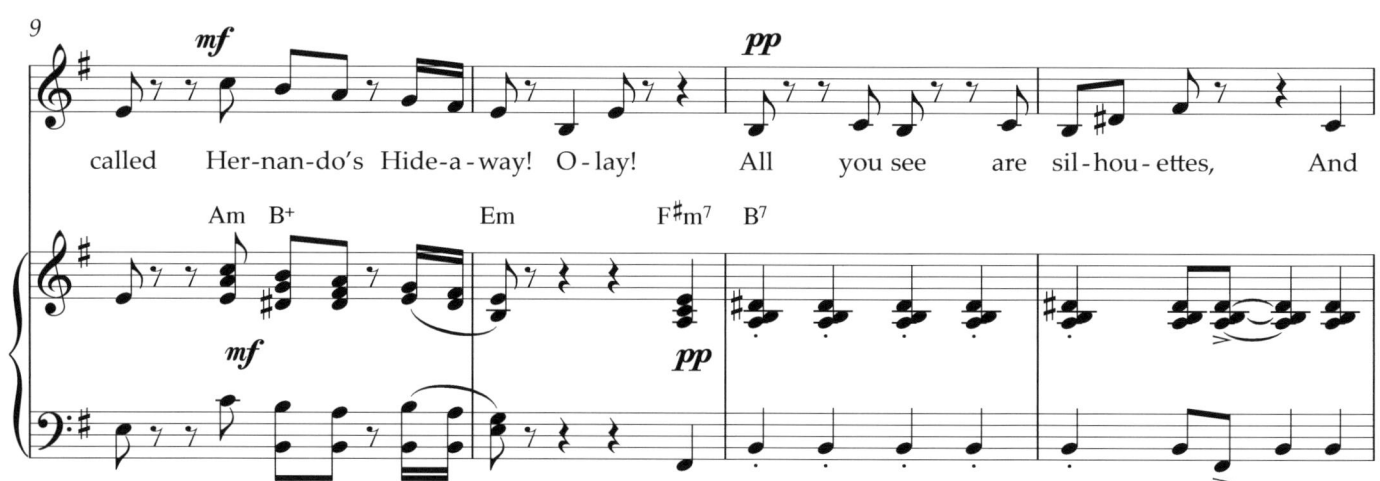

© 1954 J & J Ross Music Co and Lakshmi Puja Music Ltd
Warner/Chappell Music Ltd

42

vocal range

You're Never Fully Dressed Without a Smile

from *Annie*

Lyrics by Martin Charnin
Music by Charles Strouse
arr. Lin Marsh

© 1977 (Renewed) EDWIN H. MORRIS & COMPANY, A Division of MPL Music Publishing, Inc. and CHARLES STROUSE
Worldwide publishing on behalf of CHARLES STROUSE owned by CHARLES STROUSE PUBLISHING
(Administered by WILLIAMSON MUSIC)   All Rights Reserved   Used by Permission
www.CharlesStrouse.com

Comedy Tonight

from *A Funny Thing Happened on the Way to the Forum*

vocal range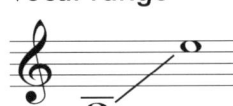

Words and Music by
Stephen Sondheim

Brightly ♩ = 104

1. Some-thing fa - mi - liar, some-thing pe - cu - liar,
2. Some-thing con - vul - sive, some-thing re - pul - sive,

Some-thing for ev - 'ry-one, a co - me - dy to - night!
Some-thing for ev - 'ry-one, a co - me - dy to - night!

Some-thing ap - peal - ing, some-thing ap - pal - ling,
Some-thing es - the - tic, some-thing fre - ne - tic,

© 1962 Burthen Music Co Inc
Warner/Chappell North America Ltd

Come Follow the Band
from *Barnum*

Words by Michael Stewart
Music by Cy Coleman
arr. Lin Marsh

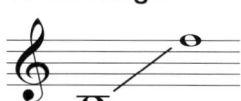
vocal range

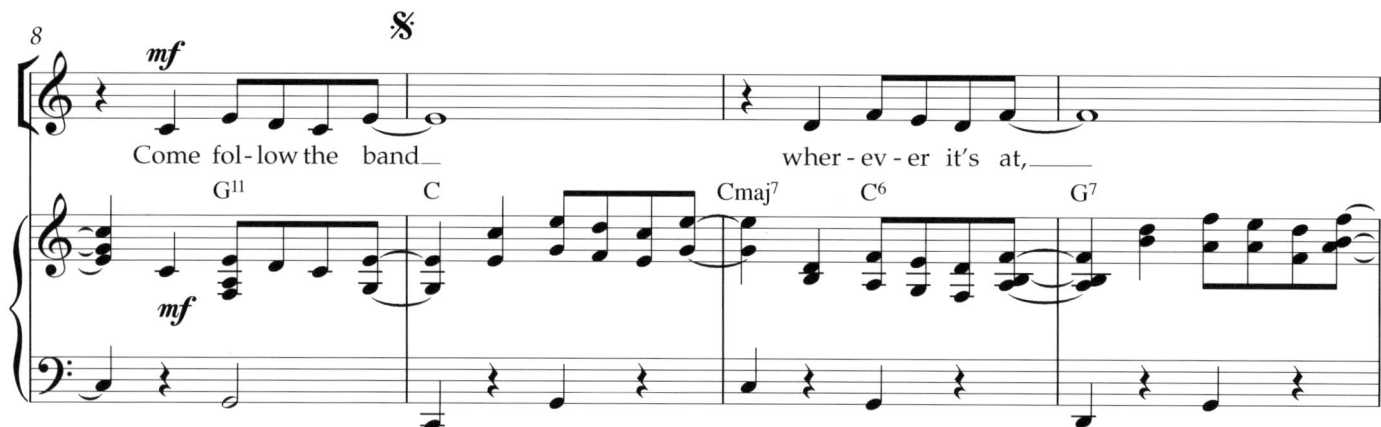

Come fol-low the band___ wher-ev-er it's at,___

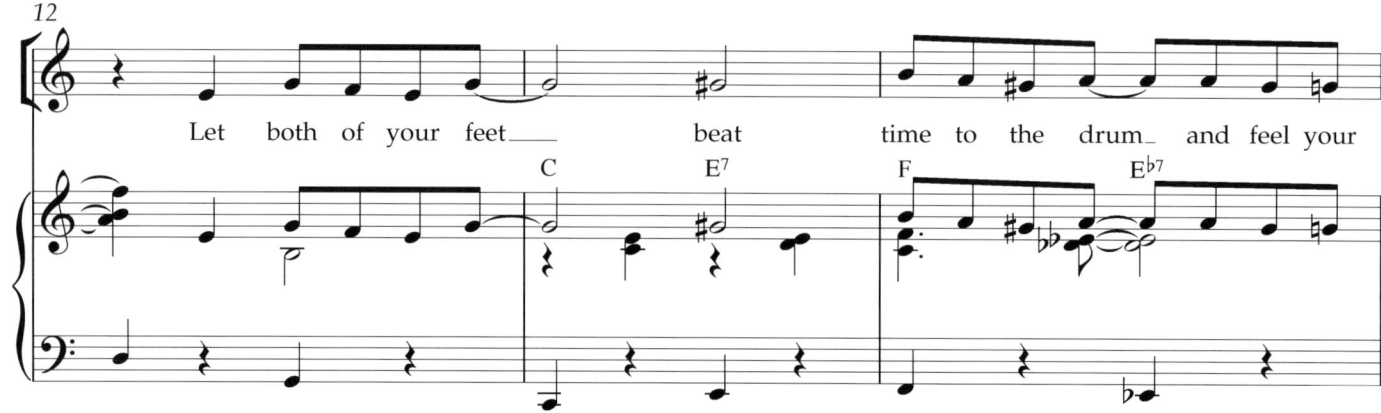

Let both of your feet___ beat time to the drum___ and feel your

© 1980 Notable Music Co Inc
Chrysalis Music Ltd

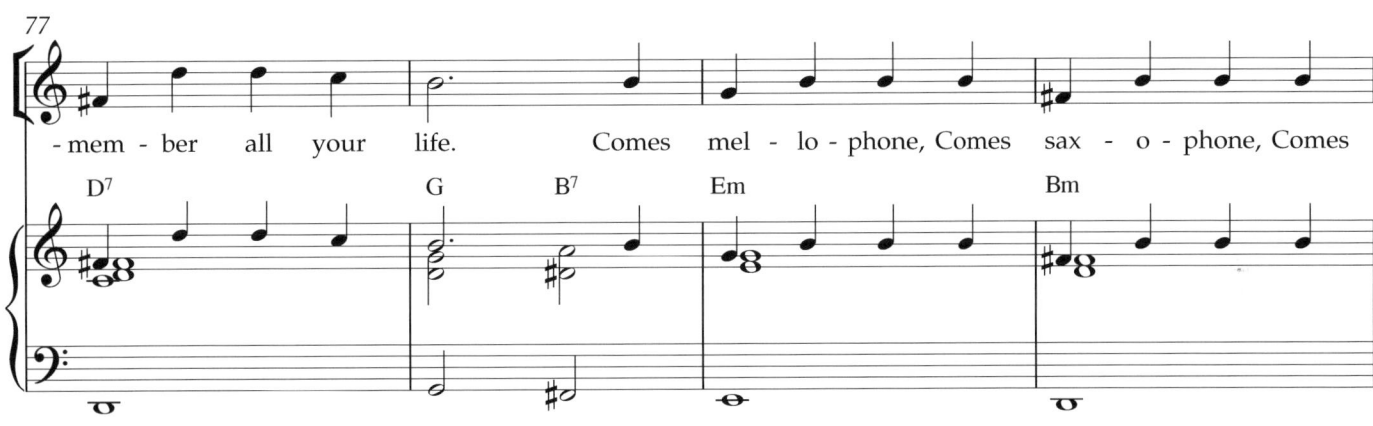

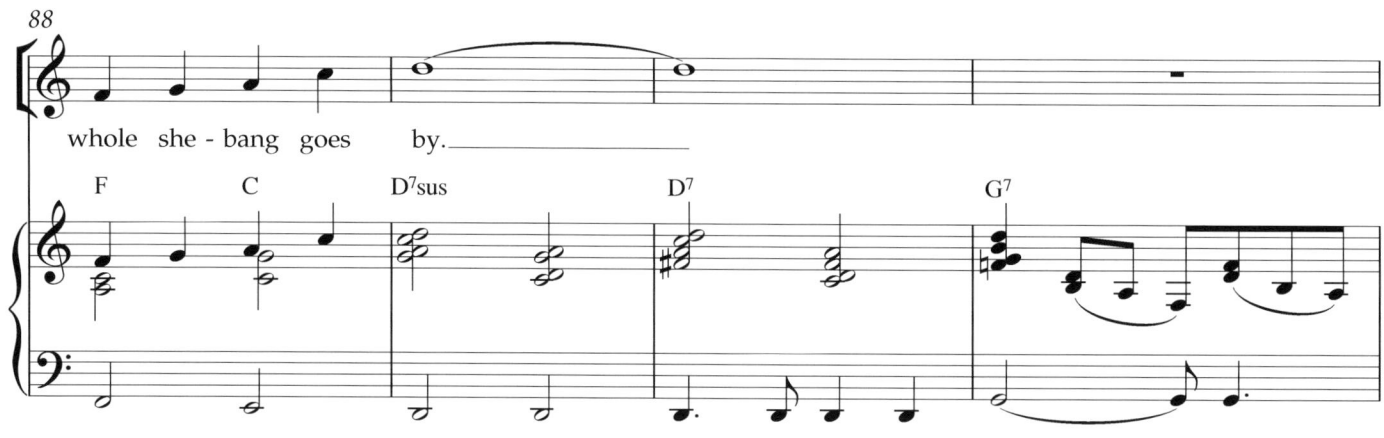

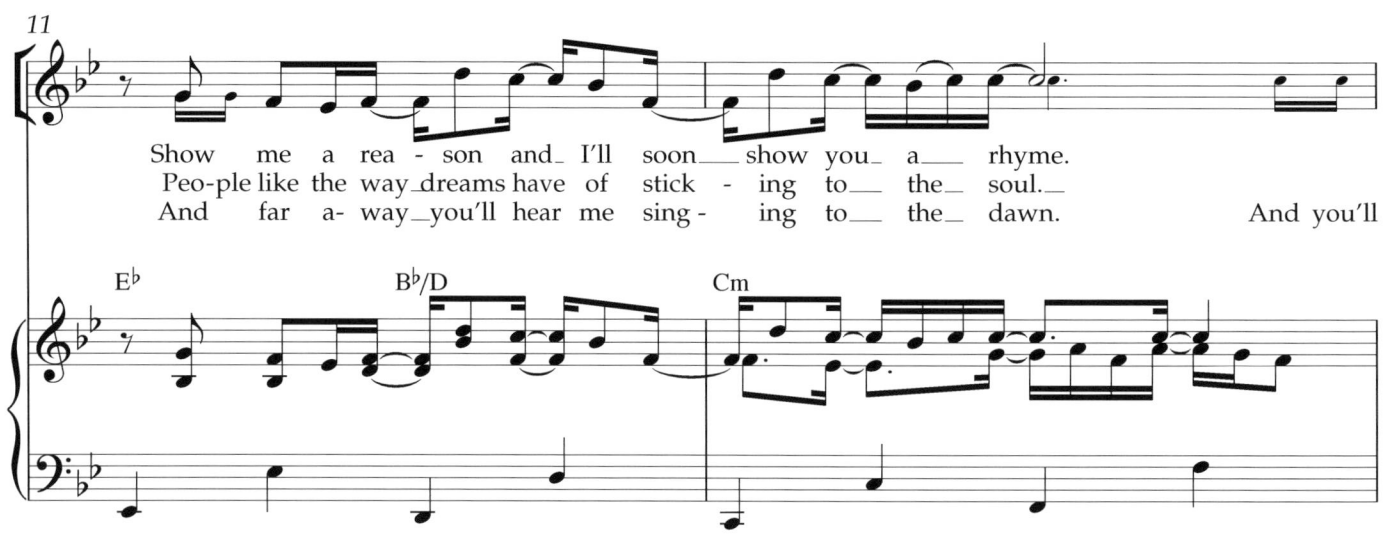

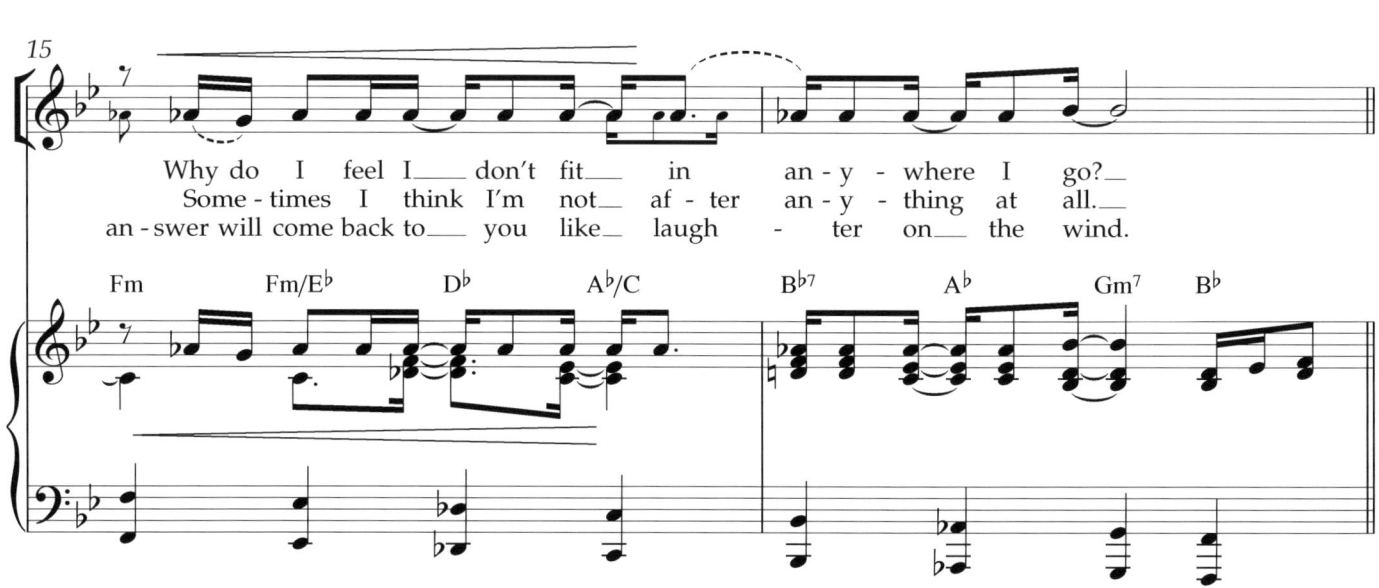

Beauty and the Beast
from *Beauty and the Beast*

Words by Howard Ashman
Music by Alan Menken
arr. Lin Marsh

vocal range

© 1991 Wonderland Music Company Inc and Walt Disney Music Co Ltd
Warner/Chappell Artemis Ltd

Seasons of Love

from Rent

Words and Music by
Jonathan Larson
arr. Lin Marsh

© 1996 Finster And Lucy Music Ltd and Universal Music Corp
Universal/MCA Music Ltd
Used by permission of Music Sales Ltd

70

And All That Jazz
from *Chicago*

Words by Fred Ebb
Music by John Kander
arr. Lin Marsh

© 1973 (renewed) Unichappell Music Inc and Kander & Ebb Inc
Warner/Chappell North America Ltd

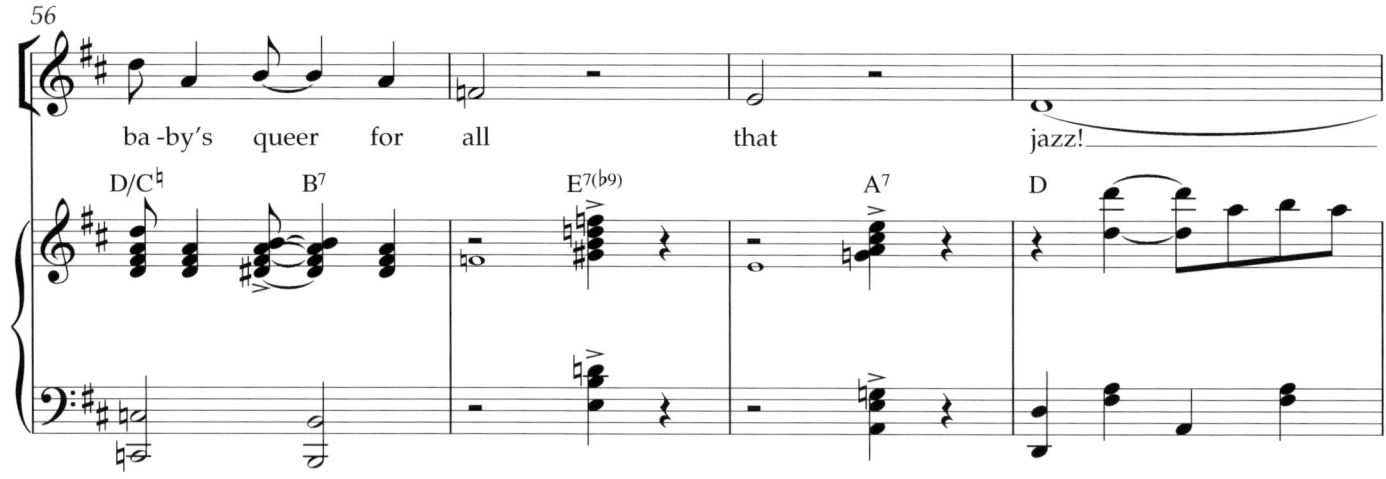

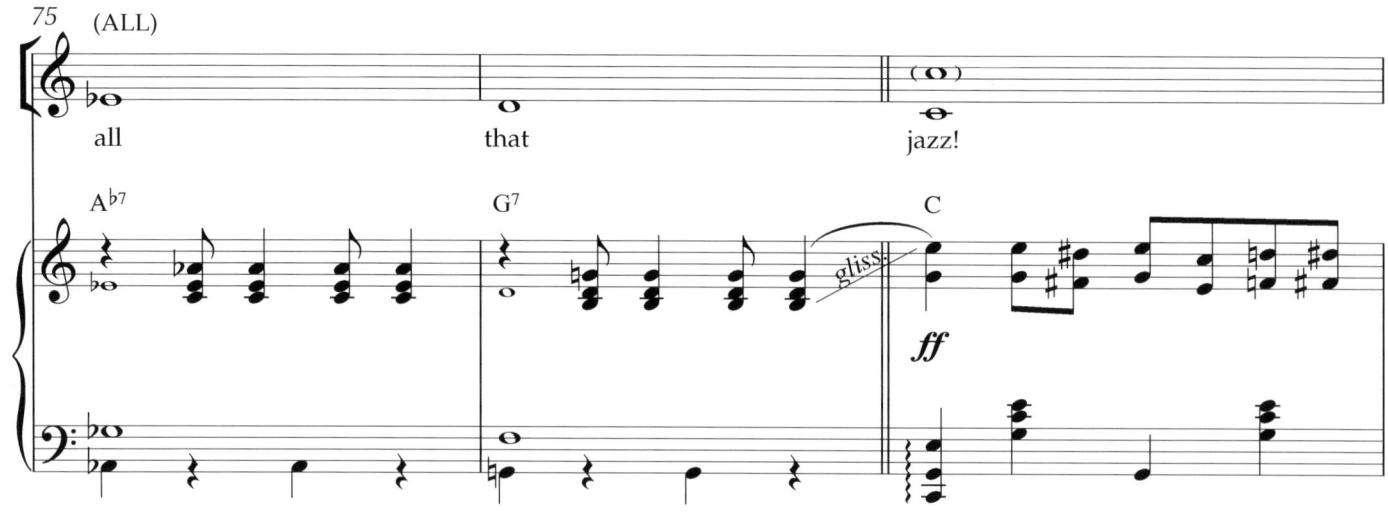

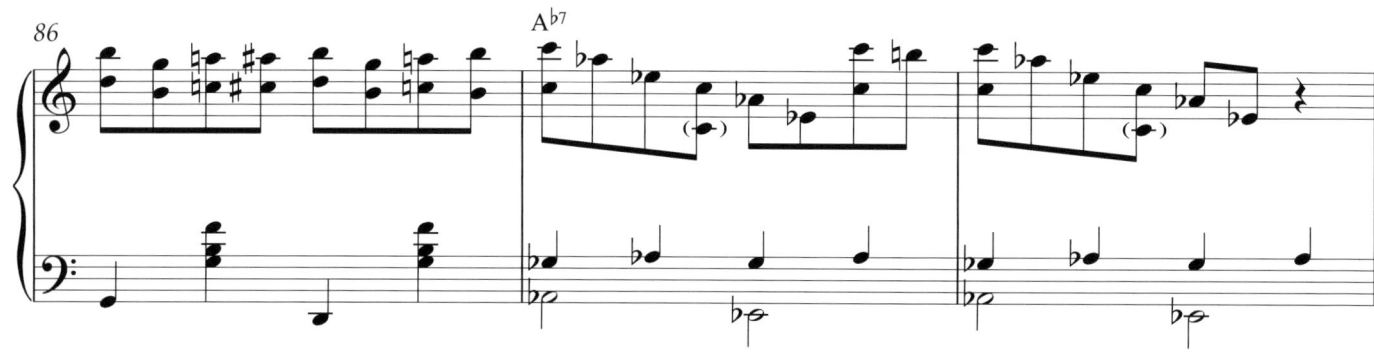

78

We Go Together
from *Grease*

vocal range

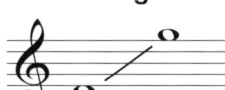

Words and Music by
Warren Casey and Jim Jacobs
arr. Lin Marsh

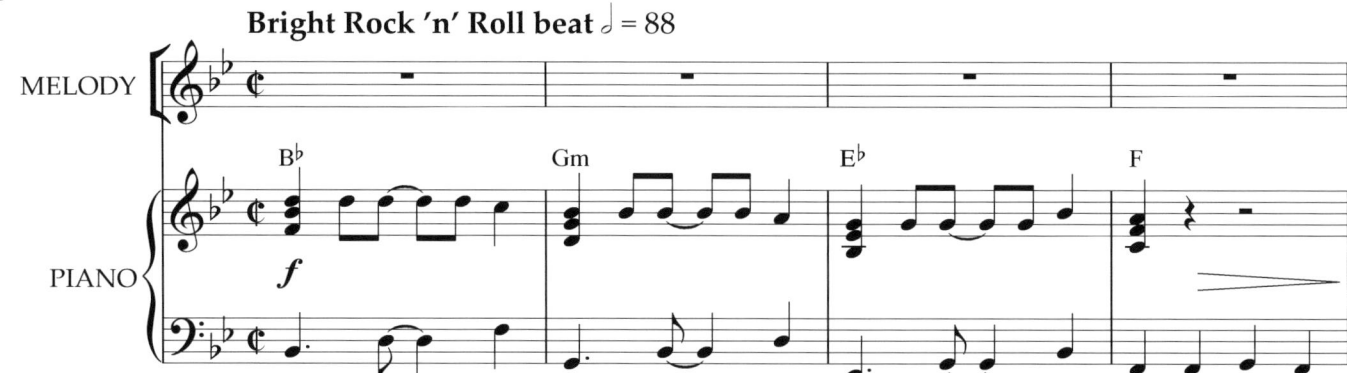

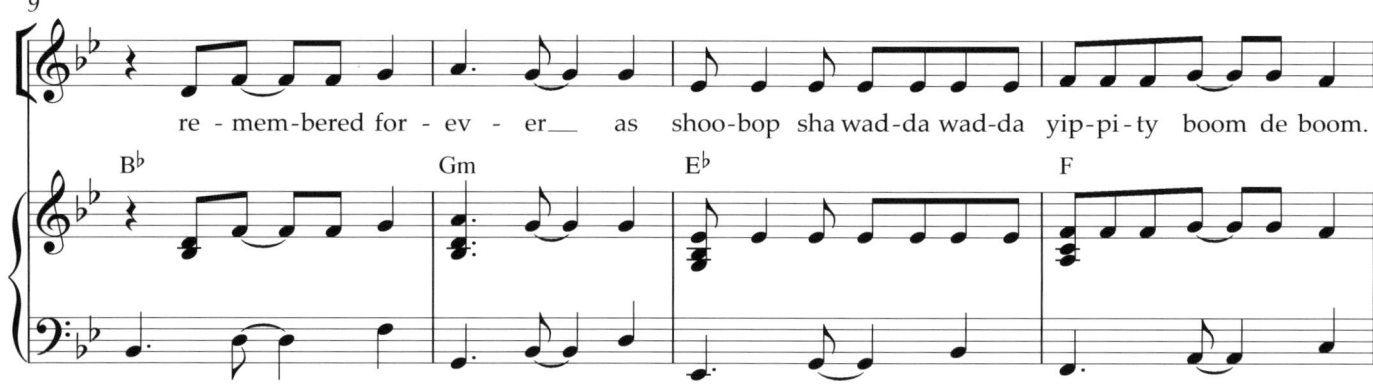

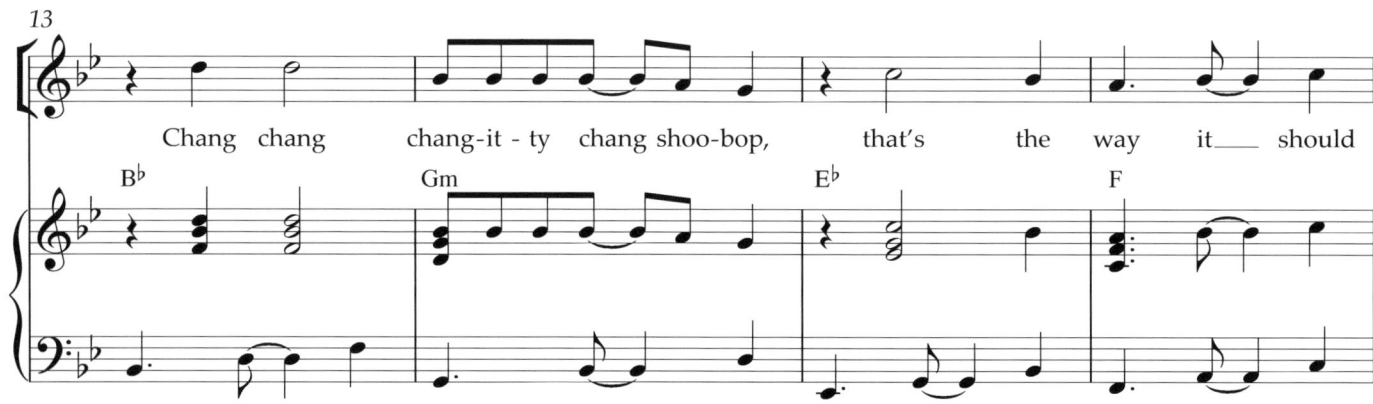

© 1978 Edwin H Morris & Co Inc
Chappell Morris Ltd

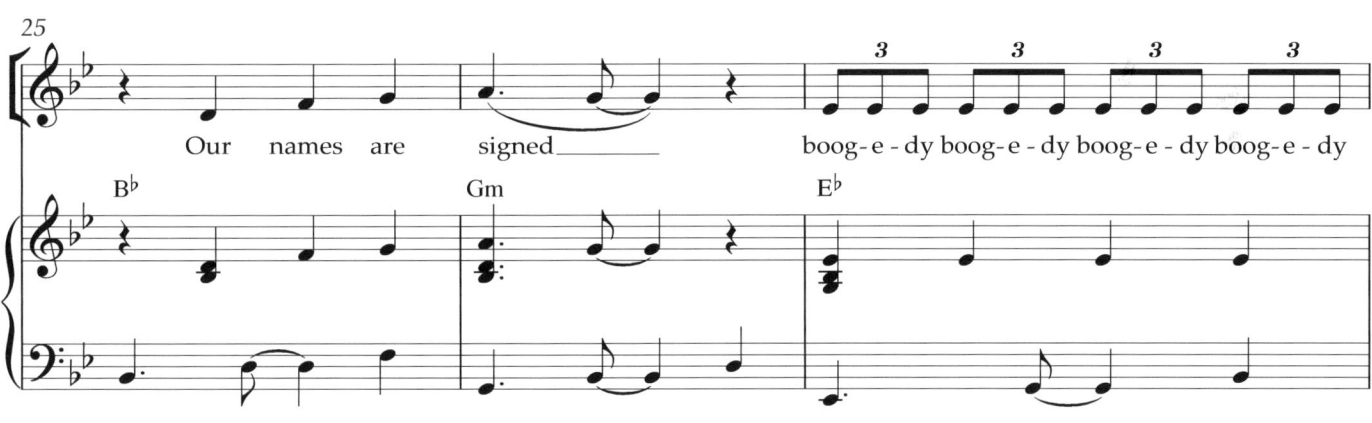

Flash, Bang, Wallop!
from *Half a Sixpence*

Words and Music by
David Heneker
arr. Lin Marsh

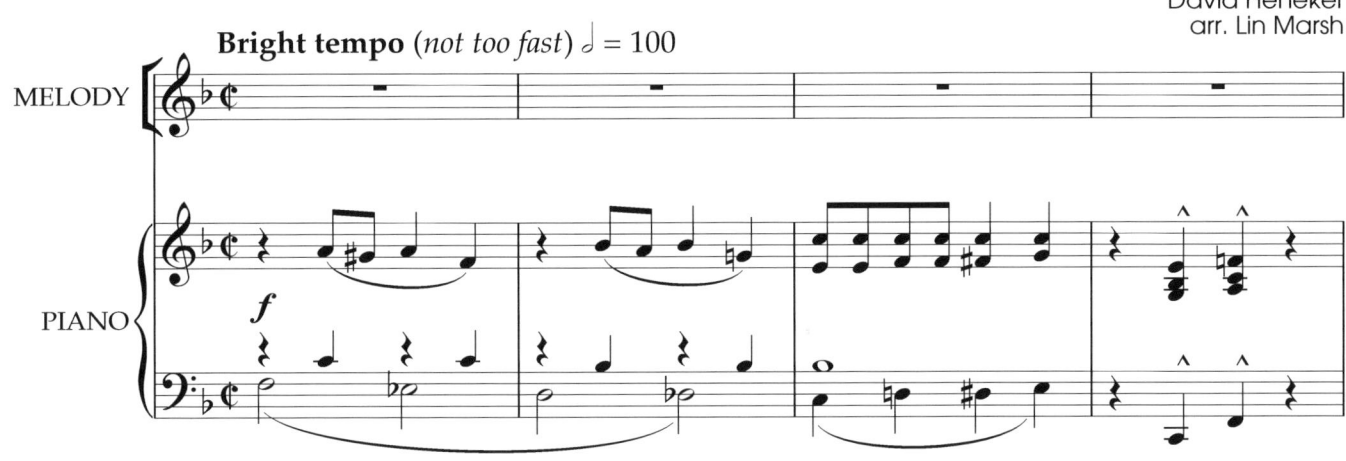

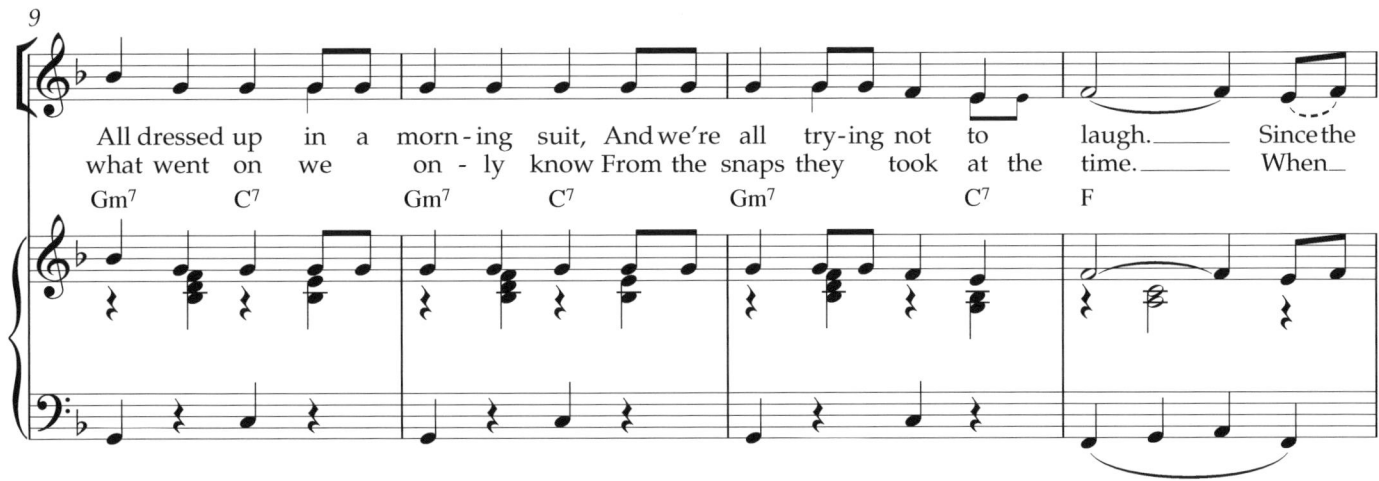

© 1965 (renewed) Chappell Music Ltd

SYNOPSES OF THE SHOWS

42nd Street
Book: Michael Stewart & Mark Bramble; Lyrics: Al Dubin; Music: Harry Warren
42nd Street is a 1933 musical film, set on the famous street in Manhattan. The Broadway musical opened in 1980, and was revived in 2001. It is set in 1933, and opens at the chorus audition for a new Broadway show, 'Pretty Lady'. This is the show that director Julian Marsh hopes will put him back on top after the devastation of the Great Depression.

The Lion King
Book: Roger Allers & Irene Mecchi; Lyrics: Tim Rice; Music: Elton John, Hans Zimmer & Lebo M
Disney's animated film was released in 1994. The musical version opened on Broadway in 1997 and features actors in animal costumes and giant puppets. *The Lion King* tells the story of a young lion in Africa named Simba, who learns of his place in the 'Circle of Life' while struggling through various obstacles to become the rightful king.

Mary Poppins
Book: Julian Fellowes; Music & lyrics: Richard M. Sherman, Robert B. Sherman, George Stiles & Anthony Drewe
The classic Disney film was released in 1964, and *Mary Poppins: The Musical* opened in London's West End in 2004. Based on the children's books by P. L Travers, Mary Poppins is an unconventional nanny who comes to live with the well-to-do Banks family in London. With the help of the cheerful chimney sweep Bert, songs and magic, Mary sets about putting the family to rights – with lots of madcap adventures along the way.

Fiddler on the Roof
Book: Joseph Stein; Lyrics: Sheldon Harnick; Music: Jerry Bock
This musical first opened in 1964 and is based on *Tevye and his Daughters* by Sholom Aleichem. A successful film adaptation followed in 1971. The play is set in the small Jewish town of Anatevka in Tsarist Russia in 1905. The story centres on Tevye, the father of five daughters, and his attempts to maintain his family and religious traditions while the world changes rapidly around him.

Cats
Book: Andrew Lloyd Webber, Trevor Nunn & Gillian Lynne; Lyrics: T. S. Eliot & Trevor Nunn; Music: Andrew Lloyd Webber
The original production of *Cats* opened in London's West End in 1981, and is based on poems by T. S. Eliot from *Old Possum's Book of Practical Cats*. It describes a particularly special night of the year when the tribe of Jellicle Cats unite to celebrate who they are. They emerge from the darkened landscape into a junkyard, singing of their unique abilities and special qualities, in the hope that they will be chosen to journey to the Heaviside layer and reborn into a new life. 'Skimbleshanks the Railway Cat' is a friendly uncle to all the cats; he attends the trains he rides, and makes sure every detail is perfect.

Cabaret
Book: Joe Masteroff; Lyrics: Fred Ebb; Music: John Kander
Cabaret the musical opened in 1966 on Broadway. It was adapted into a film by Bob Fosse in 1972, starring Liza Minelli, and is set in the Kit Kat Klub – a decadent, seedy cabaret in 1930s Berlin, during the Nazis' ascent to power. It follows the fortunes of British singer Sally Bowles and American writer Clifford Bradshaw.

The Pajama Game
Book: George Abbott & Richard Bissell; Music & lyrics: Richard Adler & Jerry Ross
This musical is based on the novel *7½ Cents* by Richard Bissell, and first opened in 1954. The story deals with labour troubles in a pajama factory, where worker demands for a seven-and-a-half cent raise are going unheeded. In the midst of this ordeal, love blossoms between Babe, the complaint committee head, and Sid, the new factory superintendent from Chicago.

Grease
Book, music & lyrics: Jim Jacobs & Warren Casey
Grease had its world theatrical premiere on Broadway in 1972, and the hit film starring John Travolta and Olivia Newton John in 1978 proved to be the highest grossing movie musical ever. Set in the summer of 1959, it tells the story of Danny Zuko, member of boy gang the T-Birds, and Sandy, an innocent girl from Australia who fall in love at the beach. Later that year the romance is revived at Rydell High School, but not without constant interference from the T-Birds, Pink Ladies and a rival gang, The Scorpions.

Singin' in the Rain
Book: Betty Comden & Adolph Green; Lyrics: Arthur Freed; Music: Nacio Herb Brown
Singin' in the Rain is a 1952 musical film starring Gene Kelly, frequently described as one of the best musicals ever made. In 1985 it was adapted from the movie into a musical for the stage. Set in 1927, Don Lockwood and Lina Lamont are the darlings of the silent silver screen. With the advent of sound in motion pictures, it is decided to turn Don and Lina's new film into a musical. The only problem is Lina's disastrous voice, and so chorus girl Kathy Selden is brought on to dub her speaking and singing voice in secret. But then Lina finds out...

Annie
Book: Thomas Meehan; Lyrics: Martin Charnin; Music: Charles Strouse
The original Broadway production of *Annie* opened in America in 1977, and is based on a comic strip called 'Little Orphan Annie'. Set in the 1930s, Annie is a fiery young orphan girl who lives in Miss Hannigan's miserable orphanage. But her hopeless situation changes when she is selected to spend time at the residence of the wealthy Oliver Warbucks. He decides to help Annie find her long lost parents by offering a reward, but an evil plan led by Miss Hannigan puts Annie in great danger.

A Funny Thing Happened on the Way to the Forum
Book: Burt Shevelove & Larry Gelbart; Music & lyrics: Stephen Sondheim
The original Broadway production opened in 1962 and was made into a film in 1966, though most of the songs were cut. *A Funny Thing Happened on the Way to the Forum* is based on the farces of the ancient Roman playwright Plautus. It tells the story of a slave named Pseudolus and his attempts to win his freedom by encouraging the romance between his master's son and a young courtesan, who is already promised to a soldier.

Barnum
Book: Mark Bramble; Lyrics: Michael Stewart; Music: Cy Coleman
Barnum opened on Broadway in 1980. A version was filmed for BBC Television in 1986, starring Michael Crawford. It is based on the life of showman Phineas Taylor Barnum, who formed the circus 'The Greatest Show on Earth'. Barnum builds a museum of curiosities supported by his wife Charity. As the years go by, Barnum is persuaded to enter politics. His colourful campaign leads to him become Mayor, but when Charity dies he leaves this lifestyle to create the biggest circus in the world.

Pippin
Book: Bob Fosse & Roger O. Hirson; Music & lyrics: Stephen Schwartz
The show opened on Broadway in 1972 and was directed and choreographed by Bob Fosse. In 1981 a stage production was filmed for Canadian television, entitled *Pippin: His life and times*. The story is loosely based on the life of Pippin, the son of Charlemagne (King Charles the Great) and his quest for an extraordinary life.

Beauty and the Beast
Book: Linda Woolverton; Lyrics: Tim Rice & Howard Ashman; Music: Alan Menken
Disney's animated film was released in 1991 and *Beauty and the Beast The Musical* officially opened on Broadway at the Palace Theatre in 1994. The tale of *Beauty and the Beast* is one of the best-known fairy stories in the world. It tells the story of a Belle, a beautiful young woman who longs for a life of adventure, and a Prince who has been turned into a hideous Beast, concealed in an enchanted castle. To break the spell, the Beast must learn to love another and earn their love in return.

Rent
Book, music & lyrics: Jonathan Larson
The rock musical *Rent* debuted in New York City in 1996 and the cinematic adaptation was released in 2005. Based on Puccini's opera *La bohème*, the musical centers on a group of impoverished young artists and musicians struggling to survive in New York's Alphabet City in the early 1990s, under the shadow of AIDS.

Chicago
Book: Fred Ebb & Bob Fosse; Lyrics: Fred Ebb; Music: John Kander
Chicago is based on the play by Maurine Dallas Watkins, and concerns the 1924 trials of two murderesses. It was first performed in 1975, with the film adaptation released in 2002. Composer John Kander and lyricist Fred Ebb modelled each song on a traditional vaudeville number or performer, emphasizing the comparison between justice, show business and contemporary society.

Half a Sixpence
Book: Beverley Cross; Music & lyrics: David Heneker
Half a Sixpence was written especially for British pop star Tommy Steele. The show transferred to Broadway in 1965 and a film version, also starring Steele, followed in 1967. It was based on H.G. Wells's novel *Kipps: The story of a simple soul*. Kipps is an apprentice draper whose life is turned upside down when he inherits a fortune. However, this creates problems which are only resolved when the fortune is lost, eventually teaching him that money can't buy happiness.

ESSENTIAL AUDITION SONGS

KIDS	**Kids**	MALE	**Broadway**
FEMALE	**Broadway**	MALE	**Pop Ballads**
FEMALE	**Jazz Standards**	MALE	**Timeless Crooners**
FEMALE	**Movie Hits**	MALE & FEMALE	**Comedy Songs**
FEMALE	**Pop Ballads**	MALE & FEMALE	**Duets**
FEMALE	**Pop Divas**	MALE & FEMALE	**Wannabe Pop Stars**
FEMALE	**West End Hits**	MALE & FEMALE	**Love Songs**

To buy Faber Music publications or to find out about the full range of titles available please contact your local music retailer or Faber Music sales enquiries:

Faber Music Ltd, Burnt Mill, Elizabeth Way, Harlow CM20 2HX
Tel: +44 (0) 1279 82 89 82
fabermusic.com